CONTENTS

Words that appear in **bold italic** in the text are explained in the glossary on page 30.

WHO WERE THE EGYPTIANS?

The *civilization* that grew up in Egypt was one of the oldest in the world. It started about 5,000 years ago and lasted for more than 3,000 years. The ancient Egyptians were descended from hunters who lived in North Africa. Gradually they learned how to grow food by planting seeds and harvesting crops. At first, there were two separate kingdoms – Upper and Lower Egypt. Then, around 3100 BC, these were united to form a single country ruled by a king, or Pharaoh. When a Pharaoh died, another member of his family became the new ruler. The Pharaohs are divided into families, called dynasties.

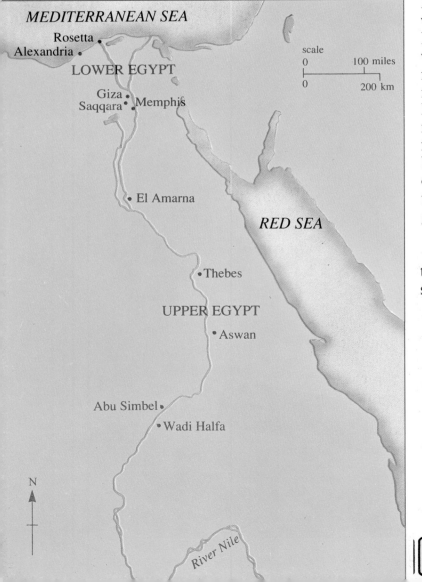

Egypt is a very hot, dry country and civilization was able to develop there only because of the River Nile. The river flooded each year and, when the floodwaters went down, a layer of mud was left on the land on either side. This mud was very *fertile* and it enabled the Egyptians to grow more food than they needed. This meant that not everyone had to farm the land, so some people could work as builders, potters, craftsmen, priests and in other jobs. It also meant that Egypt could trade the extra food it did not need for other goods that were not available in the country.

◄ This map shows many of the most important towns and cities of ancient Egypt. As you can see, they were all built beside the Nile.

THE
EGYPTIANS

Roger Coote

Wayland

Look into the Past

The Ancient Chinese
The Anglo-Saxons
The Aztecs
The Egyptians
The Greeks
The Incas
The Japanese
The Maya
The Normans
The Romans
The Sioux
The Tudors & Stuarts
The Victorians
The Vikings

Series editor: Joanna Housley
Series designer: David West
Book designer: Joyce Chester

This edition published in 1995 by Wayland (Publishers) Ltd

First published in 1993 by Wayland (Publishers) Ltd
61 Western Road, Hove, East Sussex, BN3 1JD

© Copyright 1993 Wayland (Publishers) Ltd

British Library Cataloguing in Publication Data
 Coote, Roger
 Egyptians. – (Look into the Past series)
 I. Title   II. Series
 932

PAPERBACK ISBN 0-7502-1717-0

Typeset by DJS Fotoset Ltd, Sussex, England.

Printed and bound by Eurografica, Italy

Picture acknowledgements
The publishers wish to thank the following for providing the photographs in this book: Peter Clayton 16; E.T. Archive 7 (bottom, Cairo Museum), 22 (British Museum), 29 (both); Mary Evans 5 (bottom); Werner Forman 6 (Cairo Museum), 7 (top), 8 (Cairo Museum), 9 (left, McAlpine Collection), 13 (both, Cairo Museum), 14 (bottom, Egyptian Museum, Turin), 15 (bottom, left and right), 17 (bottom), 19 (bottom, Cairo Museum), 21 (top); Robert Harding Picture Library 9 (right), 17 (top), 19 (top), 21 (bottom), 24 (bottom); Michael Holford 11 (both, British Museum), 12 (British Museum), 14 (top, British Museum), 15 (top, British Museum), 18, 20 (British Museum), 23, 24 (top, British Museum), 25 (British Museum), 26 (both; top, British Museum), 27 (both, British Museum), 28 (British Museum); Wayland Picture Library 5 (top).
Map artwork on page 4 by Jenny Hughes. Artwork on page 10 by Stephen Wheele.

▲ We know quite a lot about the Egyptians because **archaeologists** have found many remains of their civilization. Most of these remains are *tombs* in which dead people were buried. The Egyptians believed that people went on living after death, so great care was taken to bury the dead in pleasant surroundings. This tomb has been painted with scenes showing everyday life in ancient Egypt. Can you see what the people in the middle of the picture are doing? There are also pictures of some of the Egyptian gods.

◄ The tombs in which Pharaohs were buried contained the finest paintings, as well as beautiful jewellery, furniture, war chariots and other valuable items. Most of these tombs were found by robbers who stole all of the riches inside. But in 1922, an archaeologist named Howard Carter discovered a royal tomb, most of which had not been robbed. It belonged to the Pharaoh Tutankhamun and it contained more than 2,000 separate objects, many of them priceless.

RULERS AND PEOPLE

The Pharaoh was the supreme ruler of Egypt, although he gave some power to nobles and officials. The Vizier was the chief minister and judge. He controlled all aspects of the government of the country. Below him were the governors of the various areas, or 'nomes', into which the country was divided. There were also the officials of the royal court and the magistrates who tried to make sure that laws were obeyed. The army was controlled by the Pharaoh himself or his son, the crown prince. The *temples* were run by a powerful group of priests and priestesses.

◄ Egyptians regarded their Pharaohs as gods. The Pharaoh and his wife lived surrounded by great luxury, and wore the finest clothes and the most expensive jewellery. This picture shows the back of the throne found in Tutankhamun's tomb. The throne was made of wood covered with sheets of gold and silver and decorated with coloured glass and jewels. In this scene, Tutankhamun's queen is **anointing** his collar with perfume.

After the Pharaoh, the most powerful ► people in Egypt were the nobles and senior officials, many of whom were close relatives of the Pharaoh. This picture shows a nobleman and his wife. Most Egyptian men, apart from the Pharaoh, had just one wife. Although Egyptian women did not have much political power, they did have freedom and independence. Men and women had equal rights, and married women could do what they wanted with their own wealth and possessions. A man who badly treated his wife might be taken to court by her family, or his wife could divorce him.

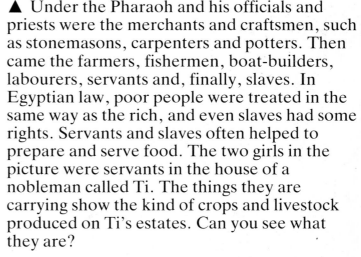

▲ Under the Pharaoh and his officials and priests were the merchants and craftsmen, such as stonemasons, carpenters and potters. Then came the farmers, fishermen, boat-builders, labourers, servants and, finally, slaves. In Egyptian law, poor people were treated in the same way as the rich, and even slaves had some rights. Servants and slaves often helped to prepare and serve food. The two girls in the picture were servants in the house of a nobleman called Ti. The things they are carrying show the kind of crops and livestock produced on Ti's estates. Can you see what they are?

LANGUAGE AND WRITING

Some of our knowledge of the Egyptians comes from their writing. They carved or painted characters, known as hieroglyphs, on monuments, walls and tombs. Hieroglyphs were also written on a type of paper called papyrus and on ostraca – pieces of stone and broken pot. Written records were kept of all business and legal matters. Most Egyptians could not read or write, however, and *scribes* were employed especially to carry out these tasks.

Hieroglyphs were a type of picture writing consisting of more than 700 different **symbols**. Each symbol represented either an object or a particular sound. Words were made up of several symbols. The picture shows some hieroglyphs that were carved and painted on the inside of the coffin of an official. The bird symbols are quails or chicks, and can also stand for the English letter 'w', while the red oval symbols represent mouths as well as sounding like the letter 'r'.

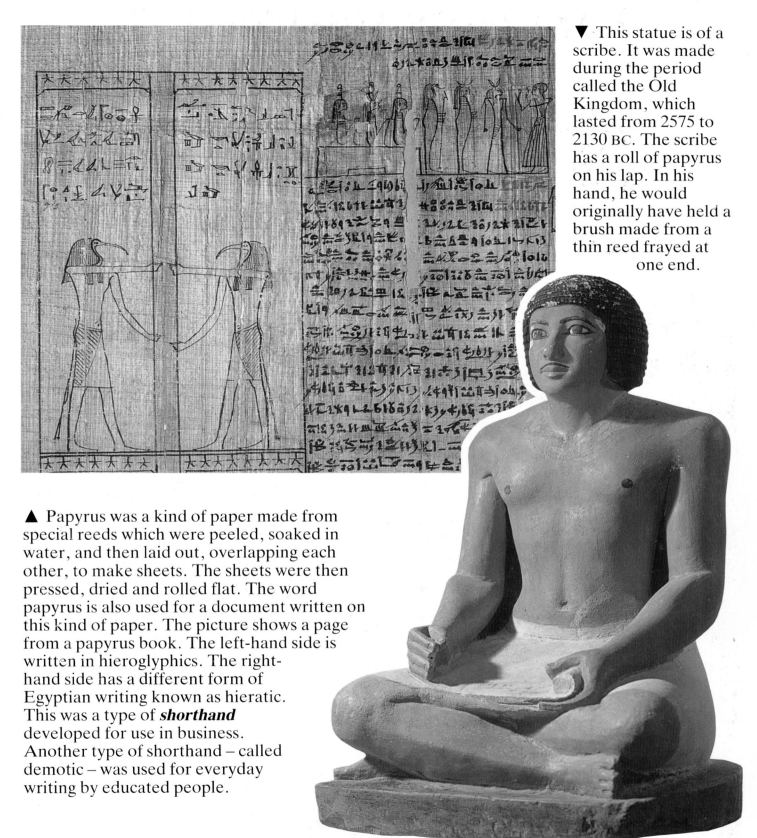

▼ This statue is of a scribe. It was made during the period called the Old Kingdom, which lasted from 2575 to 2130 BC. The scribe has a roll of papyrus on his lap. In his hand, he would originally have held a brush made from a thin reed frayed at one end.

▲ Papyrus was a kind of paper made from special reeds which were peeled, soaked in water, and then laid out, overlapping each other, to make sheets. The sheets were then pressed, dried and rolled flat. The word papyrus is also used for a document written on this kind of paper. The picture shows a page from a papyrus book. The left-hand side is written in hieroglyphics. The right-hand side has a different form of Egyptian writing known as hieratic. This was a type of **shorthand** developed for use in business. Another type of shorthand – called demotic – was used for everyday writing by educated people.

HOUSES

The large temples and some of the palaces of the Pharaohs were built using blocks of stone. The stone was *quarried* from cliffs and then dragged to the river on sledges. Boats then carried the stone to where it was needed. The houses where ordinary people lived, however, were constructed from mud-bricks. These were made from mud that was baked in the hot sun until it was hard.

Vent

Branches and straw

Mud-brick oven

Kitchen

Floors of hard-packed earth

Cellar

This illustration shows a typical house built in about 1500 BC for a workman and his family. It was built of mud-bricks and had a brick roof supported on palm tree logs. The roof above the larger rooms was held up by strong wooden columns. The walls of the most important rooms were plastered and sometimes decorated with *murals*. The house had only one storey, with steps leading up to the roof.

▲ This papyrus from around 1300 BC shows a nobleman and his wife standing in their garden. They are making an offering to the god Osiris, the god of the dead. In front of the man we can see an ornamental garden pool, and behind the couple is their house.

◄ This stone model is of a house built some time after 1000 BC. Like those of earlier times, these more modern houses were made of mud-bricks, but they were different in that they had two storeys instead of one. This made them tall and thin rather than low and narrow.

CLOTHES AND JEWELLERY

For most of the year, the weather in Egypt was hot, so clothes were quite thin. They were made of linen, a fabric produced from a plant called flax. Among wealthy Egyptians, fashions changed over time, but ordinary people wore much the same type of clothes throughout the whole period of Egyptian civilization. Men usually wore a short kilt and women wore an ankle-length tunic. In winter, when the weather was colder, people wore large cloaks made of wool.

This papyrus shows Hunefer, a wealthy Egyptian, and his wife Nasha. Both are wearing long linen tunics although Nasha's is of a finer material than her husband's. On her head, Nasha has a cone of perfumed wax. As the wax melted in the heat, it ran down the face and gave a pleasantly cool feeling. As with clothes, the hairstyles of rich people varied according to the period. Hunefer and Nasha have the elaborate hairstyles which were typical of their time, about 1310 BC.

Many Egyptians wore jewellery, especially ▶
rings and earrings, but the rich also wore
beautiful head-dresses, **pectorals** and bead
collars. This necklace and pendant was found
in the tomb of Tutankhamun. The pendant at
the bottom is in the shape of a boat carrying a
scarab beetle, which represented one
of the Egyptians' gods. The disc above
the beetle represents the sun. The
scarab and sun symbols are repeated
around the necklace.

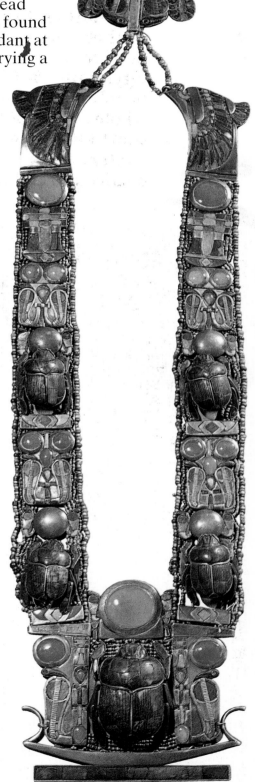

▲ Children wore their hair in a different way
from adults, as you can see here. Young boys
had their hair cut short or even shaved off
except for one long lock of hair which was left
on the side of the head. Young girls sometimes
had a number of plaits instead.

13

FARMING AND FOOD

Every July, the River Nile flooded for a few weeks. When the floodwaters went down, they left behind a layer of fertile mud. Because of this flooding Egyptian farmers were able to grow enough food to feed all the people and still leave some to be sent abroad.

◄ After the floods had gone, farmers prepared their fields by ploughing them with ploughs made of wood and bronze. The surface of the soil was then broken up with rakes, like the one at the bottom of this picture. Then seeds were sown by hand and trodden into the ground by animals which were driven across the fields. As the crops grew, weeds had to be dug out using a hoe, like the one on the left of the picture. (The other tools in the picture are a plumb bob, chisels and a hammer, which would have been used by builders.)

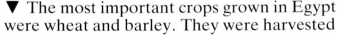

▼ The most important crops grown in Egypt were wheat and barley. They were harvested in March and April. The grain was separated from the straw by being trampled by cattle, and then taken to be stored in a ***granary***. The men in the picture are carrying grain up a ramp to the granary. Granaries were built above ground-level to protect the precious crops from rats and mice. The grain was used to make bread, which was the main food of poor people.

Farmers raised ▶
livestock on the
hillsides near the Nile.
When the crops had
been harvested, herds
of sheep, cattle, goats
and pigs were brought
down to graze on the
stubble that remained
in the fields. In this
scene, a herd of cattle
is being inspected.
Cattle were kept for
both meat and milk,
while sheep provided
meat for food and
wool for warm winter
clothing. Only rich
people could afford to
eat meat.

Sometimes the ▶
flooding of the Nile
came later than usual
and occasionally it did
not come at all. When
that happened, food
was very scarce
and many
people went
hungry. This
statue shows
a man begging
for food. He is
very thin and has
clearly not eaten for
some time.

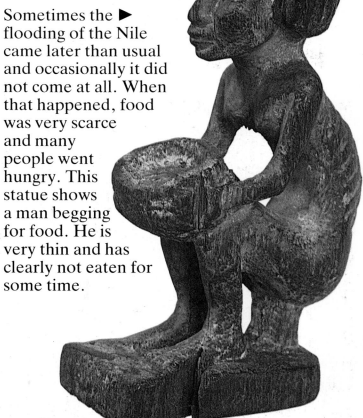

▲ Wheat and barley were not the only crops
grown. Vegetables, especially onions, were a
major part of most Egyptians' diet. Grapes
were also grown along the Nile. The men in
this picture are treading grapes to squeeze out
the juice to make wine. Ordinary people
mostly drank beer made from barley.

WORK

Because the land around the Nile was so fertile, not everyone had to work in the fields to produce enough food for the population of Egypt. This enabled people to do other kinds of work such as making pottery, building royal tombs, carpentry and boat building.

Builders were very important in Egypt. The men in this tomb painting are making mud-bricks, which were used for nearly all Egyptian buildings. The workers on the left are taking water from a pond. The water was mixed with earth and straw, and the mixture was then poured into an oblong-shaped wooden mould. When the mixture had set, the brick was turned out of the mould and left in the sun to bake until it was hard and strong enough to use for building.

▲ The craftsmen of Egypt were extremely skilful. They made beautiful jewellery, carvings, furniture and other objects. This scene from a tomb painting at Thebes shows carpenters at work. They are making furniture, probably for a tomb or the home of a nobleman or other wealthy Egyptian. Some of the men are cutting wood with saws that look rather like those we still use today. The men at the top left of the picture are smoothing and polishing a piece of wood.

This picture shows metalworkers. The painting dates from about 1450 BC and was found in the tomb of the Pharaoh Rekh-mi-re at Thebes. The craftsmen are making large copper vessels which were probably intended to be placed in the tomb with Rekh-mi-re for him to use in the afterlife (see page 27). The man to the left of centre in the picture is decorating a finished vessel by engraving a design on the surface. ▼

TRADE

Egypt was a great trading nation, and trade had been carried on with neighbouring lands since before the country was made into one nation, around 3100 BC. The main goods that were exported were *surplus* wheat and barley, linen, papyrus and rope. In return, Egypt received gold, silver, copper, ivory, jewels, spices, ostrich eggs and feathers, *incense*, timber and slaves. The Egyptians did not use money – instead goods were bartered, or exchanged for each other.

Many of the countries with which Egypt traded could be reached overland, but it was often easier to use boats because they could carry more than pack animals, such as donkeys. This ***relief*** shows an ▶ Egyptian boat of between 2600 and 2200 BC. It was probably a riverboat rather than a sea-going craft. All foreign trade was meant to be controlled by the Pharaoh, but sometimes sailors came ashore secretly to sell their goods privately.

▲ The Egyptians often used incense in their temple ***rituals***. Because incense-bearing trees did not grow in Egypt they had to be imported from the land of Punt (modern-day Somalia). The men in this picture are carrying incense trees to be loaded on to ships. The trees are being carried in baskets to protect their roots. After being unloaded in Egypt, the trees would be replanted.

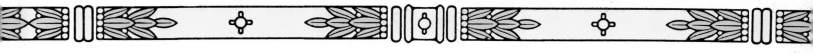

Ostrich feathers ▶ were used in ancient Egypt to make fans and decorative head-dresses. Although ostriches were found in Egypt and were hunted for their meat and feathers, extra supplies of feathers had to be imported from Nubia (part of the Sudan), to the south. This scene, from a small shrine discovered in Tutankhamun's tomb, shows Tutankhamun and his wife. The head-dress the queen is wearing is decorated with tall ostrich feathers.

LEISURE

There are many paintings and reliefs which show us how the Egyptians liked to enjoy themselves. Nobles held banquets at which large quantities of food and drink were served to guests and entertainment was provided by dancers. Music and dancing were popular with both rich and poor people, as were board games. Children played with brightly coloured leather balls, spinning tops, toy animals and dolls.

This tomb painting, dating from 1400 BC, shows musicians and dancers at a banquet. The girl in the centre is playing pipes. Other instruments used included harps, lutes, drums and tambourines. The Egyptians did not have a system for writing down their music, so it was not difficult for blind people to become musicians and singers. Several tomb paintings show blind harpists.

◄ Some dancers who were hired for banquets and other entertainments could also do acrobatics. This relief shows a group of acrobats turning somersaults. The relief was carved on the temple of Amun at Karnak. The acrobats were performing for the crowds who would have gathered to celebrate a religious holiday.

This board game ► was found in Tutankhamun's tomb. It looks rather like a long, narrow chess board, but we do not know how the game was played.

One of the most popular pastimes among the
rich was hunting. Animals such as gazelles,
antelopes, stags, ostriches and leopards were
hunted with bows and arrows. In the marshes
near the mouth of the River Nile, people
hunted duck and other water fowl. This
painting shows a nobleman hunting fowl with
his wife and daughter. The cat was used to
frighten the birds out of the reeds and then the
hunter would attempt to bring them down by
throwing a snake-shaped stick at them.

GODS AND RELIGION

The Egyptians worshipped a great many gods and goddesses, and each one could appear in a variety of forms. Temples were built for the gods and people believed the gods lived there in the form of statues. Each day, the statue inside a temple was dressed and given offerings of food and drink. The Pharaoh was thought to be the son of Amun, the king of the gods.

This photograph shows part of the huge temple complex at Karnak, on the eastern bank of the River Nile near Thebes. Constructed during the period known as the New Kingdom, which began in 1539 BC, Karnak is one of the largest religious structures ever built. It was designed to honour the most important god at that time, Amun-Re, who was a combined form of two gods: Amun, the king of the gods and Re, the sun-god.

▲ This papyrus from 1200 BC shows the god Re in his boat. Like many other Egyptian gods, Re was associated with a particular type of animal and was usually shown in the form of a man with a falcon's head. He was crowned with a disc representing the sun. Re was often linked with other gods, including Amun, Sobek the crocodile-god, and Horus the sky-god.

◄ This painted relief from the Valley of the Kings shows Osiris, the god of the dead. He was the grandson of Re and was married to Re's sister, Isis, who was called the divine mother. Osiris and Isis were two of the most popular gods in Egypt and people believed that they had once ruled the country as king and queen.

DEATH AND THE AFTERLIFE

From the time of the Middle Kingdom (1938 to 1600 BC), it was believed that everyone went on living after death (before that time, only the Pharaoh was thought to have an afterlife). When a wealthy person died, the body was taken to the *embalmers'* workshop. The embalmers took out the internal organs, including the brain and heart, and put them in special containers called *canopic jars*. The body was treated with special spices, oils and perfumes and covered with salt to preserve it and was then wrapped in linen. Seventy days later the funeral was held. During the ceremony, it was thought that the dead person's spirit crossed the River of Death and entered the Next World.

Anubis, the jackal-god, was the god of embalming. Here we can see a priest, wearing an Anubis mask, embalming the body of a nobleman called Anhai. The picture is from a papyrus which was part of Anhai's Book of the Dead. Wealthy people were buried with their own Book of the Dead, which contained a map and various magic spells that would enable them to enter the Next World by passing through gates guarded by fierce serpents.

◄ When the body of a very important person ► had been mummified (embalmed and wrapped in linen), it was placed in a decorated mummy-case. This mummy and case belonged to a priestess at Thebes, who died in about 1050 BC. The case has been beautifully painted inside and out. You can see mummies like this one in several museums around the world.

▼ Ordinary people were buried in holes dug in the sand and covered over with piles of sand. Nobles and Pharaohs were buried in special tombs. During the Old Kingdom, Pharaohs' tombs were built in the form of huge stone pyramids. Inside were chambers containing the Pharaoh's mummified body and all of the things he would need in the afterlife. These pyramids at Giza (outside Cairo) are some of the most famous in Egypt. All of Egypt's pyramids were broken into by grave robbers. In the New Kingdom, Pharaohs were buried in tombs cut from the rock at secret places in the Valley of the Kings. Even so, most of these tombs were found and robbed.

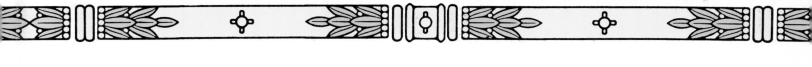

Even when Egyptians entered paradise there was work to be done in the fields. The figure in this picture was called a shabti. Shabti figures were buried with dead people and were supposed to do all the hard work in the Next World, leaving the dead free to enjoy themselves. ▼

▲ After entering the Next World, it was thought that the dead person was brought before a group of judges. He had to assure them that he had led a good life. Then the jackal-god Anubis weighed the person's heart against the Feather of Truth while other important gods looked on. In the picture, the feather is on the right-hand side of the scales, next to Anubis, and the dead person's heart is on the other side of the scales. The other gods are seated above the scales. If the heart was heavier than the feather, it meant the person had led a wicked life and would be eaten by a monster. If the heart was lighter, the person would enter a happy land and be greeted by all his dead relatives and friends.

27

WAR

Egypt was protected from most invaders by deserts and the sea. Even so, some attackers did get past these obstacles and the Egyptians had to fight to protect their country. Sometimes Egypt attacked neighbouring countries, including Nubia, Syria and Palestine. By conquering these lands, Egypt was able to obtain goods that it could not produce itself. For most of the period of Egyptian civilization, all fighting was done on land. Ships were used for carrying troops and supplies but did not take part in battles until late in the New Kingdom.

Until about 1600 BC, Egypt was not attacked by other countries. Then, people known as the Hyksos invaded their land. At that time, the weapons used by Egyptian soldiers were slings, bows and arrows, spears, daggers and axes. The Hyksos used curved swords, armour and horses and chariots. When the Egyptians managed to drive out the Hyksos they copied the weapons that had been used against them. This wall painting from the fourteenth century BC shows the Pharaoh Sethos I charging at his enemies in a two-wheeled war chariot.

This curved sword was another type of ▶ weapon copied from the Hyksos. Its handle and sheath are decorated with jewels. Most of the Egyptian army were infantrymen, or footsoldiers. Although there were horse-drawn chariots, there was no **cavalry**. The Pharaoh was the commander of the army, and he led his troops into battle.

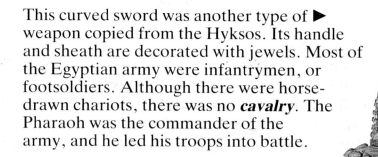

▲ This picture shows part of a decorated pavement from the Palace of Akhenaten at Tell el-Amarna. It shows an archer carrying his bow. Archers were used throughout the history of ancient Egypt. There were no guns in those days, and a bow and arrow was just about the only means of killing or wounding an enemy at long range.

GLOSSARY

Anointing Smearing oil or perfume on a person.

Archaeologists People who dig up and study objects from the past in order to learn about the civilizations that created them.

Canopic jars Vessels used for storing the internal organs of a dead person to prevent them from decaying inside the body.

Cavalry Soldiers on horseback.

Civilization A particular group of people and their way of life.

Embalmers People who prepare dead bodies for burial.

Fertile A word describing land that is good for farming because it is rich in the nutrients that plants need to help them grow.

Granary A building in which grain is stored.

Incense A substance obtained from special trees, such as myrrh trees, which gives off a strong smell when burned. It was used during religious ceremonies.

Murals Large wall paintings.

Pectoral Large pieces of jewellery that were worn around the neck and hung down across the chest.

Quarried Dug or blasted out of the ground.

Relief A carving that is done on the face of a piece of stone.

Rituals Set ways of performing religious services.

Scribes People whose job it was to write documents for others.

Shorthand A way of writing quickly, using abbreviations or symbols rather than whole words.

Symbol Something that stands for or represents something else.

Surplus What is left over after using what is needed.

Temples Buildings for the worship of goddesses and gods.

Tomb A structure built to contain the body of a dead person.

IMPORTANT DATES

Most of these dates are so long ago that historians cannot be sure of exact years. All dates are BC.

3100 Upper and Lower Egypt united into one kingdom.

2925–2575 The Early Dynastic Period.

2860 Papyrus is first used for writing.

2600 The first step pyramid built for Pharoah Djoser at Saqqarah.

2575–2130 The Old Kingdom (IIIrd–VIth Dynasties) The Great Pyramid is built at Giza during the IVth Dynasty.

2325–2150 Trading at its height.

1938–1600 The Middle Kingdom (XIth and XIIth Dynasties).
During the XIth Dynasty the Egyptian Empire grows, especially to the south.
During the XIIth Dynasty the arts flourish in Egypt.

1630–1540 Invasion of the Hyksos, and their rule of Egypt.

1539–1075 The New Kingdom: Egyptian Empire at its largest.

1332–1323 Rule of Pharaoh Tutankhamun.

950–730 XXIInd Dynasty, when Egypt is ruled by Libyan kings.

664–332 The Late Period, when Egypt is ruled by Persian and Ethiopian kings as well as Egyptian Pharaohs.

332 Alexander the Great claims Egypt for Greece. Egypt is ruled by Greece and Macedonia until it becomes part of the Roman Empire in **30 BC**.

BOOKS TO READ

Ancient Egypt by Anne Millard (Usborne, 1981)
This is a useful pocket guide to everyday life in Egyptian times.

Ancient Egypt by Robert Nicholson and Claire Watts (Two-Can Publishing, 1992)
This book mixes facts, stories and activities to give you an insight into the lives of the ancient Egyptians.

Egypt by Steve and Patricia Harrison (BBC Educational, 1990)
This book tells you all about Egypt from its ancient civilization to the modern state it is today.

Egyptian Farmers by Jim Kerr (Wayland, 1990)
This book shows you, through photographs and artwork, how farmers in Egypt made their livings.

Egyptian Pyramids by Anne Steel (Wayland, 1989)
Using artwork and photographs, this book takes you through the process of building pyramids.

Pyramids by Anne Millard (Franklin Watts, 1989)
This book deals with the everyday lives of people living in ancient Egypt.

INDEX